danceclub

linedancing

2005

danceclub

linedancing

paul bottomer

southwater

This book is dedicated to the Three Stars Dance Ranchers,
whose sense of fun is, I hope, reflected in this book as a
reminder of what dancing is all about.

———

This edition is published by Southwater

Distributed in the UK by
The Manning Partnership
251–253 London Road East
Batheaston
Bath BA1 7RL
tel. 01225 852 727
fax 01225 852 852

Published in the USA by
Anness Publishing Inc.
27 West 20th Street
Suite 504
New York
NY 10011
fax 212 807 6813

Distributed in Canada by
General Publishing
895 Don Mills Road
400–402 Park Centre
Toronto, Ontario M3C 1W3
tel. 416 445 3333
fax 416 445 5991

Distributed in Australia by
Sandstone Publishing
Unit 1, 360 Norton Street
Leichhardt
New South Wales 2040
tel. 02 9560 7888
fax 02 9560 7488

Southwater is an imprint of Anness Publishing Limited
Hermes House, 88–89 Blackfriars Road, London SE1 8HA
tel. 020 7401 2077; fax 020 7633 9499

© Anness Publishing Limited 1996, 2002

Publisher: Joanna Lorenz
Senior Editor: Lindsay Porter
Photographer: Anthony Pickhaver
Make-up and Styling: Bettina Graham
Designer: Siân Keogh

Previously published as *Dance Crazy: Line Dancing*

1 3 5 7 9 10 8 6 4 2

Contents

Introduction

The enormous popularity of American Country Line Dancing is growing and growing with an enthusiasm, energy and drive which seems unstoppable. Not only in North America, but in Europe, too, people have discovered the fun of stretchin' denim on the dance floor. The choice of the USA among Europeans as a holiday destination, coupled with inexpensive transatlantic flights, have brought more and more people into contact with Country music in the many clubs to be found in almost every American town from Florida to Washington State. The increase in popularity of Country music must also, in no small way, be due to the arrival of Country Music Television in Europe by satellite and the ever-increasing number of commercial radio stations and magazines devoted to Country music.

By the end of the eighties, Country music had begun to change, with the formerly well-defined borders becoming blurred by a cross-over of styles. Soft rock was being incorporated and the lyrics, which were once predominantly sad, simple or sugary, were now acquiring a more up-to-date and intelligent sophistication which appealed to an audience previously untouched by Country. The cowboy image of Stetsons, boots and belt buckles gradually lost its Hicktown associations and added a fun element, while

Left: The skyline of Nashville, Tennessee, undisputed centre of Country music.

Right: Interior of Grulin's, one of the leading music stores of Nashville

music videos helped to broadcast the image of what has become known as New Country.

This process was considerably aided by the emergence and promotion of new and very talented stars of the New Country music scene: Mary-Chapin Carpenter, Trisha Yearwood, Lorrie Morgan, Carlene Carter, Suzy Boguss, Michelle Wright, Shania Twain, Shelby Lynne, Ronna Reeves, Dwight Yoakum, Alan Jackson, Garth Brookes, Billy Ray Cyrus, John Berry, Vince Gill, Travis Tritt, Toby Keith, Hank Flamingo, John Michael Montgomery, Joe Diffie, Shawn Camp and a good many more. These performers realized that the music is only half of the phenomenon of Country and so produced music of an excellent quality not only for listening but also for dancing. A new phrase, the "Dance Ranch", was coined for Country music dance parties. During the eighties, attendances rocketed and more Dance Ranches were quickly established at Country & Western clubs throughout the world. Singles do not need to worry about not having a partner and the

relaxed and exuberant atmosphere ensures that everyone has a great time. The music makes you just want to dance.

American Country Line Dancing owes some of its popularity to the Disco Line Dancing of the seventies, following the Saturday Night Fever boom. However, the traditional moves of American Country dancing were not forgotten and some of them have been adapted for Line Dancing. Men in discos were never very comfortable with the idea of using their arms and dancing in the style of John Travolta, so the less ostentatious, more laid back style of Country, where thumbs are left firmly tucked in the tops of jeans, was bound to be a winner.

As its name suggests, American Country Line Dancing comprises pre-set routines of moves performed in lines. Everyone starts at the same time, dances the same steps in synchronization with everyone else (or that's the theory) and finishes with the end of the music. A lot of the music used for dancing has a moderate tempo or walking pace and most of the dances are suitable for any age group. Dancing keeps you fit and mentally alert and is a great way of making new friends. The moves are the same for both men and women and you will find that the steps often reappear in more than one dance. While, at first, the prospect of learning many line dances may seem a little daunting, as your vocabulary of moves rapidly grows, you will find new dances relatively easy to pick up by remembering the sequence of moves rather than the individual steps. The dances themselves vary in length and, therefore, may not always fit exactly with the musical phrasing but no one really seems to care. It is enough to be out there, slappin' leather and stompin' with the best of them, while you enjoy some great music.

Occasionally, a popular piece of music spawns many different dances all with the same name – the Achy Breaky is a good example. This can lead to confusion, so if you are unsure whether the dance which has been announced is the one you know, it is as well to sit out and watch the first sequence before joining in. It is not smart to dance a different dance to everyone else.

The organization of the dance party may also vary from event to event. In some clubs, an announcer may determine the choice of dance. In others it will be whoever is first on the floor who decides. Sometimes, several different dances are performed by different groups of people at the same time, although this is not recommended and a good organizer will avoid this sort of problem. The choice of the dance by the announcer is clearly more practical but, whatever circumstances prevail, the good humour of the dancers will ensure a fabulous evening's fun.

In this introduction to American Country Line Dancing, the moves are introduced as they appear in the dances and are fully explained. In some of the supporting photographs, the dancers may have their backs to you to make it easier for you to follow the moves at home.

Above: American Country Line Dancing - good exercise and boot scootin' fun.

What to Wear

Dance Ranch parties are always casual. Many Dance Ranchers opt for jeans, cowboy boots, a cowboy-style shirt or T-shirt and a Stetson-style hat. A recent fashion is for the women to wear "lacers", which are lace-up boots. Trainers or sneakers are out, as they make turns difficult and squeaky cowboys and cowgirls just ain't worth a lick. Belt buckles are always very fashionable. If you are visiting a Dance Ranch for the first time, you might feel more comfortable in just jeans and a T-shirt, as some events are more outfit-orientated than others and it will give you a chance to find out what others are wearing. On the other hand, you could just go for it. If the Dance Ranch turns out to be one of the more conservative ones, you'll be a star!

Above: Western accessories for that ranch-hand style.

Right: No dance-rancher would be seen in sneakers - cowboy boots are a must.

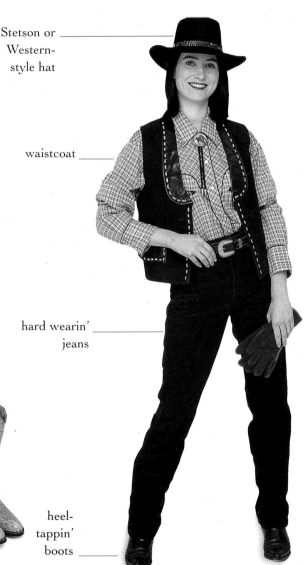

Stetson or Western-style hat

waistcoat

hard wearin' jeans

heel-tappin' boots

Getting Started

Start with the feet together facing the same way as everyone else. Be aware which move you are going to do first and ensure that you are standing on the appropriate foot. Avoid putting your hands behind your back, on your hips or down by your sides. Place your thumbs inside the waistband of your jeans or skirt, keep your steps small and you're ready to go.

ORIENTATION

In most dances, you will turn to face a new wall during the routine, as the beginning is repeated. Sometimes this is a quarter turn (or 90 degrees), sometimes it is a half turn (or 180 degrees). If you are a newcomer to American Country Line Dancing, avoid standing at the back of the dancers. You could, at the end of the dance, find yourself at the front! The middle is the safest place for the beginner. Now let's get down to some serious fun and start dancing!

USING THIS BOOK

A lot of the American Country Line Dances are danced to music with a regular 4/4 time signature and a tempo of 30 to 34 bars of music per minute, so many of the dances can be danced to a wide variety of popular music.

On the following pages you will be taught a number of the most popular American Country Line Dances. Each numbered step represents a count in the music. If a number is followed by "&" this represents a half beat. Work through the figures at your own pace – you'll soon get the hang of it!

Left: Avoid putting your hands down by your sides when dancing.

The Electric Slide

T his dance incorporates some of the basic moves common to many American Country Line Dances. The Electric Slide refers to the slide used on an electric guitar to produce the characteristic sound associated with Country music. The first move is called the Grapevine, although this is usually shortened to the Vine. The Vine is a frequent figure in many dances.

VINE TO THE RIGHT – *Start with the feet together, standing on the left foot.*

1 Move to the side with the right foot.

2 Cross the left foot behind the right foot. Start with the ball of the left foot, as this is more comfortable.

4 Tap the floor with the heel of the left foot. (Some dancers stomp or scuff this step and that's OK, too.) End standing on your right foot.

3 Move to the side with the right foot, and put your weight on it.

VINE TO THE LEFT

5 Move to the side with the left foot.

◀ **6** Cross the right foot behind the left foot.

7 Move to the side again with the left foot.

◀ **8** Tap the floor with the heel of the right foot. End standing on your left foot.

WALKING BACKWARDS TO TAP

9 Walk backwards onto the right foot.

10 Walk backwards onto the left foot.

11 Walk backwards onto the right foot.

12 Cross the left foot back across the right foot and tap.

MUSIC SUGGESTION

Enjoy the easy tempo and have fun with Joe Diffie's "Prop Me Up Beside the Jukebox" (Sony). Then you can really get moving to John Michael Montgomery's "Be My Baby Tonight" (Atlantic)

"Cotton Eye Joe", by Rednex (Internal Affairs), which topped the charts in 1995, is not mainstream Country, but is a faster version which you can have some fun with.

STEP TAPS

13 Walk forward onto the left foot.

Style Tip

Steps 9–11: It is the sign of a good dancer to step backwards onto the heels, releasing the toes and "fanning" the toes out to the side, but this may take a little practice.

Step 14: It is good style to incline the left side forward and tip your hat – even if you don't have one!

14 Tap the right foot across and behind the left foot. Turn the right knee out a little to make it easier.

15 Walk backwards onto the right foot.

16 Cross the left foot back across the right foot and tap.

THE SCUFF

18 Swing the right leg forward so that the right heel scuffs the floor. As you do this, pivot on the left foot and make a quarter turn to the left. Don't put your right foot down. To maintain balance, make sure that you hold your body weight over your left foot and do not allow it to follow the scuffing foot.

Start the dance again facing the wall that was previously on your left. You are now dancing the Electric Slide.

17 Walk forward onto the left foot and flex the knee slightly.

Slappin' Leather

This next dance uses nearly all the elements of the Electric Slide, then moves on to introduce some more classic Country Dance moves. Slappin' Leather starts with a Vine to the Right, a Vine to the Left and Walking Backwards to Tap of the Electric Slide. Start with your feet together, facing the front, having completed steps 1–11 of the Electric Slide.

THE TAP

12 Cross the left foot back across the right foot and tap.

SLIDES

▼13 Walk forward onto the left foot.

14 Slide the right foot to close to the left foot.

15, 16 Repeat Steps 13 and 14.

HEEL SPLITS – *Now you are standing on the balls of both feet with the feet almost together.*

17 "Fan" both heels to open out.

▼18 "Fan" both heels in to close.

19, 20 Repeat Steps 17 and 18.

FORWARD AND BACKWARD DOUBLE TAPS

23, 24 Moving the right foot backwards, tap twice with the toe.

21, 22 Moving the right foot forward, tap twice with the heel.

STAR

25 Standing on the left foot, point the right foot forward.

26 Standing on the left foot, point the right foot out to the side.

▲ **27** Standing on the left foot, point the right foot backwards.

28 Standing on the left foot, point the right foot out to the side.

MUSIC SUGGESTION

"Baby It's You", by Hank Flamingo (Giant), is particularly popular for this dance. Another real favourite is Shania Twain's "You Win My Love" (Mercury).

SLAPPIN' LEATHER

30 Swivelling a quarter turn to the left on the left foot, keep the right knee flexed and move the right foot to your side at knee height. Slap your boot with your right hand.

29 Lift and move the right foot across in front of you and slap your boot with your left hand.

End standing on your left foot ready to start again. You will now be facing the wall that was previously on your left.

Southside Shuffle

Then his is a great dance for first-time Dance Ranchers. It's short and simple and you get to use some great Country moves, as well as a new way to "slap leather". The dance introduces Toe Fans, a different kind of Star from the one danced in Slappin' Leather and the by now familiar Vine. Start as usual facing the front, standing on the left foot with the feet a little apart.

TOE FANS

◀ **1** Standing on the left foot, keep the right heel in contact with the floor and "fan" the toe out to the side.

▶ **2** "Fan" the right toe back to its original position, roughly parallel with the left foot.

3, 4 Repeat Steps 1 and 2.

FORWARD AND BACKWARDS DOUBLE TAPS

5, 6 Standing on the left foot, tap the right heel forward twice.

7, 8 Standing on the left foot, tap the right toe backwards twice.

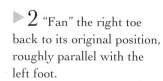

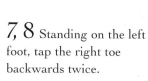

STAR AND SLAP LEATHER – *This is a different Star from the one encountered in Slappin' Leather.*

9 Standing on the left foot, point the right foot forward.

10 Point the right foot backwards.

11 Point the right foot out to the side.

12 On the left foot, cross the right foot behind and, with your left hand, slap leather!

VINES TO THE RIGHT AND LEFT WITH SCUFF AND TURN

13–20 Dance steps 1–3 of the Vine to the Right as we did in the Electric Slide. On 4, scuff the left foot. Now repeat the move to the left but on 4, when you scuff, make a quarter turn left on the left foot.

VINE TO THE RIGHT WITH SCUFF AND TURN —

21–24 Step to the side with the right foot. Cross the left foot behind the right foot. Step to the side again with the right foot. Scuff the left foot forward, while swivelling a quarter turn to the right on the right foot.

MARKING TIME TURNING TO THE RIGHT ———

25–28 On these steps, make a gradual half turn to the right: mark time with the left foot, then the right foot, then the left again. On step 28, tap the floor with the right heel.

MUSIC SUGGESTION

"Wild Man", by Ricky Van Shelton (Columbia).

Ski Bumpus

One of the difficulties encountered by many people at first is remembering the order of the moves. In the Ski Bumpus, each of the dance sections is repeated, giving you extra thinking time. You will also learn some new moves common to many American Country Line Dances. Start, as usual, facing the front with your feet together.

RIGHT AND LEFT FOOT TAPS

1 Tap the right foot out to the side.

2 Close the right foot to the left foot and stand on the right foot.

3 Tap the left foot out to the side.

4 Close the left foot to the right foot and stand on the left foot.

5–8 Repeat Steps 1–4.

MUSIC SUGGESTION

"**A** Little Less Talk and a Lot More Action", by Toby Keith (Mercury) is a good one to start with. "Honky Tonk Moon", by Rosie Flores (Hightone) is a little faster but has a great swing.

KICK BALL CHANGES – *This can be a little tricky at first but let's kick it!*

9 Flick the right foot forward from the knee.

9& Bring the right foot back and stand on it without lowering the heel. At the same time, pick up the left foot. (It is best to lift the foot only slightly off the floor.) (Count – &)

SPOT TURN TO THE LEFT

13 Walk forward onto the right foot and stand on it, leaving the left foot behind still touching the floor.

14 Standing on the right foot, swivel a half turn to the left and transfer your weight forward onto the left foot.

15–20 Repeat Steps 9–14.

▶**10** Replace the left foot to the floor and stand on it

11, 11 & , 12 Repeat Steps 9, 9&, 10.

At first, it may seem a little odd to start a turn to the left with the right foot and this turn will also seem quite fast. However, if you keep the forward step short and ensure that the toes of your left foot remain on the floor during the turn, it is impossible to turn the wrong way. As far as the speed is concerned, just relax. It is worth practising this move as it is found in many of the American Country Line Dances.

TRIPLE STEPS

▼**21** Move forward with the right foot, turning slightly to the left and with the right side leading.

▶ **21&** Using only the ball of the left foot, move the left foot towards the right foot.

> The Triple Steps, too, are common to many American Country Line Dances. The pattern is, after the Spot Turn to the Left, you are standing on the left foot and your right foot is free to lead the first Triple Step.
> NB: when a Triple Step starts with the right foot, the right foot stays in front. When it starts with the left foot, it is the left foot that stays in front.

Style Tip

The hottest way to dance a stylish Triple Step is to lift a little on the standing foot at the start and lower into the Triple Step. With a right foot Triple Step, you would lift a little on the left foot. With a left foot Triple Step, you would lift a little on the right foot. Then dance Step 15 using the ball of the foot first, before moving onto the flat foot. Note that in Step 16, only the ball of the foot is used.

▶ **22** Move the right foot forward.

23, 23&, 24 Repeat Steps 21, 21&, and 22 starting with the left foot and turning slightly to the right.

25, 26 Repeat Steps 13 and 14.

27–32 Repeat Steps 21–26.

COWBOY REGGAE – *This very popular move is also known as the "Jazz Box" and the "Coca-Rola"*

33 Cross the right foot over the left foot. If you swivel a little on the left foot, you will find the move easier and more comfortable.

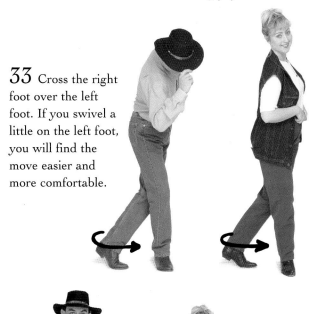

34 Move backwards onto the left foot.

35 Move to the side with the right foot.

36 Move forward onto the left foot.

37–39 Repeat Steps 33–35.

40 Close the left foot to the right foot and stand on it.

The Ski Bumpus is now complete and you are ready to start again. In some clubs, the Ski Bumpus is danced in facing lines. In this formation, you will exchange places with the dancer opposite you during the Triple Steps. When this happens, be sure to pass right side to right side first, then left side to left side. If you don't, enjoy making a new acquaintance when you bump!

Honky Tonk Stomp

The next dance uses the Vine that you learnt in the Electric Slide but with a Hitch Turn for real Dance Ranchers. You will also learn the popular Stomp. This is a great dance, especially for newcomers to American Country Line Dancing. The routine is quite short, easy to remember and the honky tonk music just makes you want to dance. Start with the feet slightly apart, standing on the left foot and facing the front. We begin with the Toe Fans first learnt in the Southside Shuffle.

TOE FANS

1 Standing on the left foot, keep the right heel in contact with the floor and "fan" the toe out to the side.

▶ 2 "Fan" the right toe back to its original position, roughly parallel with the left foot.

3, 4 Repeat Steps 1 and 2.

FORWARD AND BACKWARDS DOUBLE TAPS

5, 6 On the left foot, tap the right heel forward twice.

7, 8 On the left foot, tap the right toe back twice.

TAPS AND STOMPS

9 Tap the right heel forward.

10 Close the right foot back to the left foot and stand on the right foot.

▶ 11, 12 Stomp the left foot, lifting the knee and placing the foot down flat on the floor twice.

13 Tap the left heel forward.

14 Close the left foot back to the right foot and stand on the left foot.

15, 16 Stomp the right foot twice.

VINE TO THE RIGHT

17 Move to the side with the right foot.

18 Cross the left foot behind the right foot.

19 Move to the side with the right foot.

20 Tap the left foot.

VINE TO THE LEFT WITH HITCH TURN

21 Move to the side with the left foot.

22 Cross the right foot behind the left.

23 Move to the side with the left foot.

▶ 24 Standing on the left foot, swivel a half turn to the left. At the same time, raise the right knee, making a right angle at the ankle. This is call the Hitch.

MUSIC SUGGESTION

"Honky Tonk Attitude", by Joe Diffie (Columbia) is a real honky tonkin' number for stompin'. Another great track is The Tractor's version of "Baby Likes to Rock It" (Arista) – this is guaranteed to get you moving.

25–28 Repeat Steps 17–20.

29–31 Repeat Steps 21–23.

32 Tap the right heel, with the feet apart.

Now begin the dance again with the Toe Fans, starting with the right foot.

Tennessee Twister

T he Tennessee Twister will really get you moving, with some twists and a new type of turn. This dance is still very suitable for new Dance Ranchers. You will be dancing to the right as the dance progresses, so leave extra space on the right of the floor. As usual, start facing the front, with your feet a little apart and your weight evenly distributed over the balls of both feet.

TENNESSEE TWISTS

▼ **1** Twist on the balls of both feet, moving the heels to the right.

▲ **3** Twist on the balls of both feet, moving the heels to the left.

2 Hold the position.

4 Hold the position.

5–8 Now twist right, left, right, left. End on the left foot.

FORWARD-BACKWARDS DOUBLE TAPS

▼ **9,10** Tap the right heel forward twice.

▲ **11,12** Tap the right toe back twice.

CROSSES, STARTING WITH THE RIGHT FOOT

13 Move forward onto the right foot.

14 Cross the left foot loosely behind. It is more comfortable if you turn the left knee out and use only the ball of the left foot.

15,16 Repeat Steps 13 and 14.

SWIVEL TURN TO THE RIGHT

17 Move forward onto the right foot, flexing the knee for stability.

18 Standing on the right foot, swivel a half turn to the right. If necessary, use the left foot to steady yourself after the turn but do not stand on the left foot.

CROSSES, STARTING WITH THE LEFT FOOT

19 Move forward onto the left foot.

20 Cross the right foot behind.

21,22 Repeat Steps 19 and 20.

SWIVEL TURN TO THE LEFT

23, 24 Step forward onto the left foot, flexing the knee for stability. Standing on the left foot, swivel a half turn to the left. If necessary, use the right foot to steady yourself after the turn but do not stand on the right foot.

VINE TO THE RIGHT WITH HITCH TURN AND VINE TO THE LEFT

25–32 You now complete the dance simply by dancing the familiar Vine to the Right with a Hitch Turn making a half turn to right on the right foot and a Vine to Left.

MUSIC SUGGESTION

"Close but no Guitar", by Toby Keith (Mercury), is a slow track offering a gentle introduction to the dance. "Get in Line", by Larry Boone (Columbia), is a classic with an easy tempo to start with. Then get twistin' with Mary-Chapin Carpenter's "Right Now" (Columbia).

You can now enjoy dancing the Tennessee Twister.

The Cowboy Strut

Another very easy dance, this one is also known as the Country Strut or the Cowboy Reggae, so don't get confused if your club uses another name – the steps are the same. Here, we introduce two new figures, the Montana Kick and the Cowboy Strut, which gives the dance its name. You will already know the Cowboy Reggae from the Ski Bumpus. Start facing the front, standing with the weight on the left foot and with feet together.

HEEL TOES

1 Standing on the left foot, tap the right heel forward.

MUSIC SUGGESTION

"Fastest Healing Wounded Heart", by Michelle Wright (Arista).

▲ **2** Standing on the left foot, tap the right toe to close (without weight).

3,4 Repeat Steps 1 and 2.

5 Repeat Step 1.

6 Close the right foot to the left foot and stand on the right foot.

7–12 Repeat Steps 1–6, standing on the right foot and doing heel to toe movements with the left. Still standing on the right foot, tap the left toe to close. Finish standing on the right foot.

MONTANA KICK

13 Move forward onto the left foot.

14 Kick the right foot forward from the knee.

15 Close the right foot to the left foot.

◀ **16–19** Tap the left toe behind, then vine to the left.

20 On the left foot, swivel a half turn to the left and scuff the right foot.

COWBOY STRUTS AND COWBOY REGGAES

▶ **21&** Transfer your weight to the right foot.

22 Standing on the right foot, place the left heel forward.

22& Transfer your weight forward to the left foot.

23, 23&, 24 Repeat Steps 21, 21&, and 22.

▲ **21** Still standing on the left foot, place the right heel forward.

25–28 Dance the Cowboy Reggae.

29–32 Repeat steps 25–27 making a gradual quarter turn to the right.

Cajun Beat

Let's really get moving, as the tempo increases and we move into up-beat Country with an easy and fun-to-do dance. Popularly known as the Cajun Beat, this dance really has nothing to do with the completely different Cajun dance style. Start facing the front with the feet slightly apart and standing on the left foot.

1,2 Stomp the right foot twice. (Counts - slow, slow)

◀ 3 Move the right foot backwards. (Count - quick)

▶ 4 Move the left foot to the side. (Count - quick)

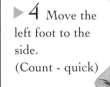

▲ 5 Walk onto the right foot.(Count - slow)

6—10 Repeat Steps 1–5 starting with the left foot and moving to the right on Step 3–5. The counts are the sam

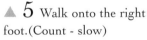

MUSIC SUGGESTION

The music for the Cajun Beat is terrific and the atmosphere can get really ballistic as everyone starts stompin' like a good ole boy.

"Down at the Twist and Shout", by Mary-Chapin Carpenter (Columbia), is tremendous fun.

"Guitar Talk", by Michelle Wright (Arista), is another stompin' great.

11 Walk forward onto the right foot, leaving the left foot in place. (Count- slow)

12 Rock back onto the left foot. (Count - slow)

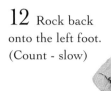

13 Walk forward onto the right foot. (Count - quick)

▶ **14** Cross the left foot behind the right foot. Turn the left knee out a little and use only the ball of the left foot. (Count - quick)

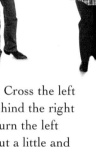

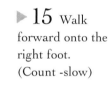

▶ **15** Walk forward onto the right foot. (Count -slow)

16–20 Repeat Steps 11–15 starting with the left foot.

WALKS AND TRIPLE STEPS – *For 21–28, make a half turn to the right.*

21 Walk forward onto the right foot. (Count - slow)

22 Walk forward onto the left foot. (Count - slow)

23 Step forward with the right foot, turning to the left. (Count - quick)

23& With the ball of the left foot, move the left foot to the right. (Count - quick)

24 Step forward with the right foot, leading with the right side. (Count - slow)

25 Walk onto the left foot. (Count - slow)

26 Walk forward onto the right foot. (Count - slow)

27, 27&, 28 Repeat Steps 23, 23& and 24, starting with the left foot and turning to the left. (Counts - quick, quick, slow)

End standing on the left foot. After the half turn to the right, you will be facing the wall which was previously behind you.

I Feel Lucky

Occasionally, when a dance is devised with a particular piece of music in mind, the dance takes the same name as the music track. This popular dance is performed to the hit "I Feel Lucky" (Columbia). Start facing the front, with your feet together and standing on the left foot.

WALKING BACKWARDS AND FORWARD TO TAP AND CLAP

1 Walk backwards onto the right foot.

2 Walk backwards onto the left foot.

3 Repeat Step 1.

▶ 4 Tap the left foot and clap your hands.

5 Walk forward onto the left foot.

6 Walk forward onto the right foot.

7 Repeat Step 5.

▶ 8 Tap the right foot and clap your hands.

TURN TO THE RIGHT

▶ 9 Making a quarter turn to the right, walk forward onto your right foot.

▶ 10 Making a quarter turn to the right along the same line, step to the side onto the left foot. You now have your back to the front.

11 Making a half turn to the right along the same line, step to the side onto the right foot. You are now facing the front.

12 Tap the left foot on the floor and clap hands.

TURN TO THE LEFT

13–16 Repeat Steps 9–12, making the turns to the left and moving the opposite foot.

> During the Turns to the Right and Left, ensure that you keep your feet apart and that you always track in the same direction to avoid turning back on yourself.

POINTS, TAPS AND CLAPS

17 Step onto the right foot.

18 Point the left foot forward.

19 Point the left foot to the side.

WALKS AND CROSS

29 Walk forward onto the right foot.

30 Walk forward onto the left foot.

▼ **31** Cross the right foot over the left.

▲ **20** Hold the position and clap your hands.

21–23 Repeat steps 17–19 starting with the left foot.

24 Hold the position and clap your hands.

25 Step onto the right foot.

26 Point the left foot forward and clap.

27, 28 Repeat Steps 25 and 26 starting with the left foot.

32 Step back onto the left foot.

> You are now ready to start again.

Tush Push

This is one of the most popular dances in the Country & Western clubs. It is slightly more complicated than the dances encountered so far, but if you dance it slowly until you have got the pattern and feel of it, you will be able to join the crowd as you and they enjoy the Tush Push. Start facing the front, with your feet apart and standing on your left foot.

HEEL PRESSES

1–4 Standing on the left foot, tap the right heel on each count. On count 4, transfer your weight to the right foot.

5–8 Tap the left heel on each count. On count 8, transfer your weight to the balls of both feet.

TWISTS

9–11 With your weight on the balls of both feet, twist to the left, to the right and to the left again.

12 Hold the position and clap.

DOUBLE AND SINGLE HIP BUMPS

This is the sequence that gives the dance its name. You are now standing on the left foot with the feet apart.

◀ **13** Transfer your weight onto the right foot and push through the right hip.

14 Relieve the pressure for a moment, then repeat Step 13. This is a Double Hip Bump to the right.

15–16 Repeat Steps 13 and 14 to dance a Double Hip Bump to the left, using the left foot and the left hip.

17–20 Dance Single Hip Bumps to the right, the left, the right and the left. End on the left foot.

CHA CHA CHA AND CHECKS

This movement is danced to a Cha Cha Cha rhythm which is a count of 1, &, 2. It is a little similar to a Triple Step. Avoid using your heels in these moves and in the Checks.

21 Move the right foot forward. (Cha)

21& Close the left foot towards the right foot, with the foot turned out and only using the ball of the foot. (Cha)

22 Move the right foot forward. (Cha)

23 Check forward onto the left foot, leaving the right foot in place behind.

24 Replace your weight back onto the right foot

25 Move the left foot backwards. (Cha)

25& Close the right foot towards the left foot. If you prefer, you can cross the right foot loosely in front of the left foot. (Cha)

26 Move the left foot backwards. (Cha)

27 Check backwards onto the right foot, leaving the left foot in place in front.

28 Replace your weight forward onto the left foot.

29, 29&, 30 Repeat Steps 21, 21& and 22.

SPOT TURN TO THE RIGHT

31 Walk forward onto the left foot and stand on it, leaving the right foot behind still touching the floor.

MUSIC SUGGESTION

Many Country music tracks have a Cha Cha Cha rhythm which makes them suitable for this dance.

"Kiss Me in the Car", by John Berry (Liberty), is very catchy and the beat is easy to follow.

"She's in Love with the Boy", by Trisha Yearwood (MCA), is a big hit at Dance Ranches, and is sure to get you moving on the dance floor.

Shania Twain's catchy "I'm Outta Here" (Mercury) is a great number to push your tush to.

"Hard Times and Misery", by Travis Tritt (Warner Bros.), has an eight-bar intro and is a little slower for beginners.

32 Standing on the left foot, swivel a half turn to the right…

32 (continued)
...and transfer your weight forward onto the right foot.

FORWARD CHA CHA CHA _____

33 Move the left foot forward. (Cha)

33& Close the right foot towards the left foot, with the foot turned out and only using the ball. (Cha)

34 Move the left foot forward. (Cha)

SPOT TURN TO THE LEFT _____

35 Walk forward onto the right foot, leaving the left foot behind in place.

36 Standing on the right foot, swivel a half turn to the left and transfer your weight forward onto the left foot.

37 Walk forward onto the right foot.

38 Make a quarter turn to the left onto the left foot.

39 Stomp the right foot.

40 Hold the position on the left foot and clap.

You are now ready to start the dance again, facing the wall that was previously on your left.

T.C. Electric Slide

As time goes by, dances may develop as Dance Ranchers add new or extra moves. This development of the popular Electric Slide uses many of the same moves but introduces Jumps, Slides and Hip Bumps. Listen to the announcer to avoid confusion with the original Electric Slide.

JUMPS AND MARKING TIME

1–12 The T.C. Electric Slide starts with the first 12 steps of the original Electric Slide. You are now standing on your right foot with the left foot having tapped back and across the Right Foot.

13 Jump in place with the feet apart.

▲14 Jump in place, closing the feet.

15 Mark time by stepping in place with the left foot.

16 Mark time by stepping in place with the right foot.

Style Tip

Steps 15,16: Instead of marking time, you can perform a stylish movement called the Scissors. Jump in place, crossing the right foot in front. Jump again, crossing the left foot in front.

SLOW SLIDES

17, 18 Slide the left foot slowly forward.

19, 20 Slide the right foot to close with a tap.

21, 22 Slide the right foot forward.

23, 24 Slide the left foot to close with a tap.

DOUBLE AND SINGLE HIP BUMPS, TURN AND SCUFF

25, 26 Move the left foot to the side and double hip bump to the left.

▶ **27, 28** Transfer your weight to the right foot and double hip bump to the right.

29–31 Single hip bump to the left, the right and the left.

32 Standing on the left foot, swivel a quarter turn to the left and scuff the right foot.

> You are now ready to start again, facing the wall that was previously on your left.

Boot Scootin' Boogie

This is one of my favourite American Country Line Dances. It is quite easy, though the Boot Scoot may seem tricky at first. Start facing the front with your weight on both feet and with the feet slightly apart ready to twist.

TWISTS MOVING TO THE LEFT

▼ **1** Standing on the heels of both feet, move the toes to the left.

2 Standing on the balls of both feet, move the heels to the left.

3, 4 Repeat Steps 1 and 2.

TWISTS MOVING TO THE RIGHT

▲ **5** Standing on the balls of both feet, move the heels to the right.

6 Standing on the heels of both feet, move the toes to the right.

7, 8 Repeat Steps 5 and 6.

TOE HEELS IN PLACE

9 Standing on the left foot, lift the right heel and point the right toe to the floor.

▶ **10** Lower the right heel and stand on the right foot.

11 Lift the left heel and point the left toe to the floor.

12 Lower the left heel and stand on the left foot.

KICKS, CLOSE, POINT, CLOSE

13,14 Kick the right foot forward from the knee twice.

15 Close the right foot to the left foot.

16 Point the left foot behind.

17 Close the left foot to the right foot and stand on the left foot.

HITCH

18 Standing on the left foot, raise the right knee, making a right angle at the ankle.

TRIPLE STEPS

19, 19 & 20 Dance a triple step forward, starting with the right foot (see Ski Bumpus).

21, 21 & 22 Dance a triple step forward, starting with the left foot.

SPOT TURN TO THE LEFT

23 Walk forward onto the right foot, leaving the left foot behind in place.

24 Standing on the right foot, swivel a half turn to the left and transfer your weight forward onto the left foot.

TRIPLE STEPS

25–28 Dance a right foot then a left foot triple step as before.

MUSIC SUGGESTION

"No One Needs to Know", by Shania Twain (Mercury), is a super track to start with.

BOOT SCOOTS

29, 30 Hop forward on the left foot with the foot lightly skimming the floor and the right foot extended in front with the foot at a right angle to the leg. To assist this move, the right foot is drawn back towards the left foot as the left foot skims forward. It is a good idea to keep the left knee flexed. Repeat.

VINE TO THE RIGHT

31 Move to the side with the right foot.

32 Cross the left foot behind the right foot.

33 Move to the side again with the right foot.

POINTS AND CLAP

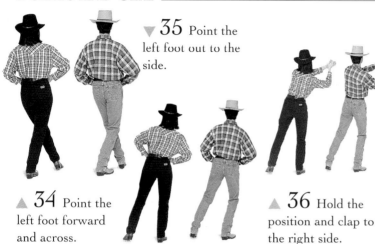

▼ **35** Point the left foot out to the side.

▲ **34** Point the left foot forward and across.

▲ **36** Hold the position and clap to the right side.

VINE TO THE LEFT

37 Move to the side with the left foot.

38 Cross the right foot behind the left.

39 Move to the side with the left foot.

POINTS AND CLAP

40 Point the right foot forward and across.

41 Point the right foot out to the side.

42 Hold the position and clap to the left.

STROLL – *This new move is just strolled through, keeping the steps small.*

43 Walk forward onto the right foot, making a quarter turn to the right.

▶ **44** Cross the left foot behind the right, releasing the heel of the right foot.

45 Walk forward onto the right foot.

46 Almost close the left foot to the right foot.

> You are now ready to start the Boot Scootin' Boogie again, but facing the wall that was on your left when you started the dance.

Sixteen Step

Many of the dances covered so far have been danced to a regular Line Dancing tempo. Now it's time to hot up the pace with a terrific dance that can be danced singly or in twos or threes. To start, everyone stands in a circle facing in an anti-clockwise direction. The dancers in front will have their backs to you and you will have your back to the dancers behind you. The circle doesn't need to be single file, so you can dance alongside your friends.

1 Standing on the left foot, tap forward with the right heel.

▼5 Standing on the right foot, tap forward with the left heel.

6 Close the left foot to the right foot and stand on the left foot.

▲2 Close the right foot to the left foot, leaving your weight on the left foot.

3 Tap forward with the right heel.

4 Close the right foot to the left foot and stand on the right foot.

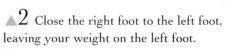

▼**7** Tap the right toe across and behind the left foot.

8 Close the right foot to the left foot and stand on the right foot.

▼**9** Standing on the right foot, tap forward with the left heel.

10 Close the left foot to the right foot and stand on the left foot.

11 Stomp with the right foot.

12 Stomp with the right foot.

13 Walk forward onto the right foot, leaving the left foot behind in place.

14 Standing on the right foot, swivel a half turn to the left and transfer your weight forward onto the left foot.

15, 16 Repeat steps 13 and 14

TRIPLE STEPS

17, 17&, 18 Dance a triple step, starting with the right foot (see Ski Bumpus).

19, 19&, 20 Dance a triple step, starting with the left foot.

21–24 Repeat Steps 17–20.

MUSIC SUGGESTION

"Sold (The Grundy County Auction Incident)", by John Michael Montgomery (Atlantic), is a masterpiece of Country music and one which I bid you enjoy.

"Man, What a Woman", by Shawn Camp (Reprise), is relaxed but excellent.

And if "Dance" by Twister Alley (Mercury), doesn't make you want to dance, I don't know what will.

Houston Slide

Slightly unusually, this dance incorporates a turn to the right. Start facing the front with feet together standing on the left foot.

TAPS AND SLIDES

▷ **1** Tap the right toe out to the side.

▷ **2** Close the right foot to the left foot, keeping your weight on the left foot.

▽ **3** Move to the side with the right foot.

▷ **4** Slide the left foot to the right foot.

5–8 Repeat starting on the left foot

FORWARD AND BACKWARDS DOUBLE AND SINGLE TAPS

9, 10 Tap the right heel forward twice.

11, 12 Tap the right toe backwards twice.

13 Tap the right heel forward once.

14 Tap the right toe backwards once.

STEP SCUFFS ────────────

15 Step forward onto the right foot.

▲**16** Standing on the right foot, swivel a quarter turn to the right and scuff the left foot.

17 Step forward onto the left foot.

18 Scuff the right foot forward.

COWBOY REGGAE ────────────

19 Cross the right foot over the left foot. If you swivel a little on the left foot, you will find the move easier and more comfortable. Tip your hat.

20 Step backwards onto the left foot.

21 Tap the right foot to the side.

▲ **22** Jump forward onto both feet to bring them together.

> You are now facing the wall which was previously on your right and you are ready to start the Houston Slide again.

Bubba

Bubba is just another name for someone who in Country parlance is euphemistically called a "good ole boy" Start facing the front with your feet together and standing on the left foot. "Boogie til the Cows Come Home" by Clay Walker (Giant) is a fine choice for this dance.

FORWARD TAP AND CLOSE

1 Tap the right heel forward.

2 Close the right foot to the left foot.

TWISTS

3 Standing on the balls of both feet, twist the heels to the right.

◀4 Twist the heels to the left.

5 Twist the heels to the right.

6 Twist the heels to the centre.

RIGHT HOOK

7,8 Tap the right heel forward. Close the right foot to the left.

▶ **9,10** Tap the right heel forward. Cross the right foot across the left knee.

11 Tap the right foot forward.

12 Close the right foot to the left foot and end standing on both feet.

13–16 Repeat Steps 3–6.

17, 18 Tap the left heel forward. Cross the left foot across the right knee.

19,20 Tap the left heel forward. Cross the left foot across the right knee

STEP TAPS

21 Walk forward onto the left foot.

22 Tap the right foot across and behind the left foot. Turn the right knee out a little to make it easier.

23 Step backwards onto the right foot.

24 Cross the left foot back across the right foot and tap.

25–28 Repeat Steps 21–24.

TURN AND STOMP

29 Walk forward onto the left foot.

30 Standing on the left foot, swivel a quarter turn to the left and stomp the right foot.

BACKWARDS WALK AND TWO STOMPS

31 Walk backwards onto the right foot.

32 Walk backwards onto the left foot.

33, 34 Stomp the right foot twice.

> You have now successfully completed the Bubba and are ready to start again.

Flying Eights

Here's a great dance using some of the moves you are already familiar with. This time, start facing the front with your feet together but standing on the right foot.

VINES TO THE LEFT AND THE RIGHT WITH HITCHES AND CLAPS

1 Move to the side with the left foot.

2 Cross the right foot behind the left foot.

3 Move to the side with the left foot.

▶ **4** Hitch the right foot and clap.

5 Move to the side with the right foot.

6 Cross the left foot behind the right foot.

7 Move to the side with the right foot.

◀ **8** On the right foot, swivel a quarter to the right, hitch the left foot and clap.

VINE TO THE LEFT WITH A THREE-QUARTER TURN AND HITCH

9–11 Repeat Steps 1–3.

12 On the left foot, swivel three-quarters to the left, hitch the right foot and clap.

STEP HITCHES

13 Walk forward onto the right foot.

14 Walk forward onto the left foot.

15 Walk forward onto the right foot.

16 Hop forward on the right foot and hitch the left foot.

17 Walk forward onto the left foot.

18 Hop onto the left foot; hitch the right.

19, 20 Repeat Steps 15 and 16.

> Now you can start again.

Cotton Eye Joe

This is one of the most popular dances and it couldn't be simpler. It can be danced individually, with a partner or in groups. Start in a circle facing anti-clockwise, as for the Sixteen Step, and standing on the left foot.

1 Tap the right heel forward.

▶ 2 Hook the right foot across in front of the left knee.

◀ 3, 3&, 4 Dance a backwards triple step, starting with the right foot

5 Tap the left heel forward.

6 Hook the left foot across in front of the right knee.

▼ 7, 7&, 8 Dance a backwards triple step, starting with the left foot.

9–16 Repeat Steps 1–8.

17–32 Dance eight forward triple steps, starting with the right foot.

MUSIC SUGGESTION

"Cotton Eye Joe", by Rednex (Internal Affairs) is the obvious choice.

Go back to the beginning and you're dancing the Cotton Eye Joe.

Cowboy Cha Cha

Earlier we mentioned the cross-over experienced in Country music and now here is an example of a dance cross-over, where Country has borrowed the cha cha cha from Latin American dancing. Start facing the front with your feet together and standing on your right foot. Remember that there are no heels in the cha cha cha movements – just slide the feet.

FORWARD CHECK AND BACKWARDS CHA CHAS

1 Check forward onto the left foot, leaving the right foot in place behind.

3 Move back onto the ball of your left foot. (Cha)

2 Move your weight backwards onto the right foot.

3&, 4 Bring the right foot back towards to the left foot. (Cha) Move back onto the left foot. (Cha)

CHA CHA TO THE RIGHT WITH A HALF TURN TO THE LEFT

As you dance Steps 5–8, make a half turn to the left.

5 Check back onto the right foot, leaving the left foot in place.

6 Move your weight forward onto the left foot.

▼ **7** Start turning to the left and step to the side with the right foot. (Cha)

▶ **7&** Still turning to the left, half close the left foot to the right

8 Still turning to the left, step to the side with the right foot to complete the half turn to the left. (Cha)

CHA CHA TO THE LEFT WITH A HALF TURN TO THE RIGHT – *As you dance Steps 9–12, make a half turn to the right.*

9 Check back onto the left foot, leaving the right foot in place in front.

10 Move your weight forward onto the right foot.

11 Start turning to the right and step to the side with the left foot. (Cha)

11& Still turning to the right, half close the right foot to the left foot. (Cha)

12 Still turning to the right, step to the side with the left foot to complete a half turn to the right. (Cha)

13 Check back onto the right foot, leaving the left foot in place.

14 Move your weight onto the left foot.

15 Start turning to the left and step to the side onto your right foot.

15& Still turning to the left, half close the left foot to your right foot.

16 Still turning, step to the side onto the right foot, completing a quarter turn.

SPOT TURNS TO THE RIGHT —

17 Walk forward onto the left foot, leaving the right foot in place.

18 On the left foot, swivel a half turn to the right and transfer your weight forward onto the right foot.

19, 20 Repeat Steps 17 and 18.

MUSIC SUGGESTION

Because of the Cha Cha rhythm, you can use the same type of music as was suggested for the Tush Push.

You are now ready to start again with the Cowboy Cha Cha.

Cowboy Partner Cha Cha

Some Line Dances are also popular as partner dances. You will find that many dancers prefer to dance on their own, while others choose the partner version of a particular dance.

The steps of the Cowboy Partner Cha Cha are identical to those of the Cowboy Cha Cha. The man stands on the woman's right. His left arm extends across her back and he takes her left hand in his. He holds her right hand in his right hand at the same height from the floor as the left hands.

As the dancers turn, the man moves from his position on the woman's right to her left and then back again. When they get to the Spot Turns, the man releases hold with his left hand. He lifts his right hand above his head on the first turn. On the second turn, the woman lifts her right hand above her head. On the four counts of the Spot Turns, the right hand will therefore move up, down, up, down. The down movement helps the turn. As the dance starts again, the partners rejoin left hands.

The Achy Breaky

So popular was the Achy Breaky Heart hit by Billy Ray Cyrus when it was first released that immediately scores of Line Dances were devised for it. The official version was choreographed by one of America's leading Line Dance choreographers, Melanie Greenwood, and here is our interpretation of her dance. Start by facing the front and standing on the left foot.

VINE TO THE RIGHT

1 Move to the side with the right foot.

◄ 2 Cross the left foot behind the right foot.

3 Move to the side with the right foot.

4 Hold the position on the right foot with feet apart.

HIP SWINGS

5 Swing the hips from the right foot to the left foot with feet apart.

6 Swing the hips from the left foot to the right foot.

◄ 7 Swing the hips from the right foot to the left foot.

8 Hold the position on the left foot.

FOOT TAPS TURNING TO THE LEFT

9 On the left foot, tap the right toe behind.

10 Tap the right toe out to the side.

11 On the left foot, swivel a quarter turn to the left and tap the right foot to the side.

12 On the left foot, swivel a half turn to the left and step back onto the right foot.

MUSIC SUGGESTION

"Achy Breaky Heart", by Billy Ray Cyrus (Phonogram).

WALKING BACKWARDS TO HITCH AND SWING STEP TO THE SIDE

13 Walk backwards onto the left foot.

14 Walk backwards onto the right foot.

15 Hitch the left foot.

16 Swing the left leg backwards, making a quarter turn to the left and end on the left foot with feet apart.

WALKING BACKWARDS TO STOMP

17 Walk backwards onto the right foot.

18 Walk backwards onto the left foot.

19 Walk backwards onto the right foot.

20 Stomp the left foot.

HIP SWINGS

21–24 Repeat Steps 5–8.

TURNING STOMPS

▼ **25** Making a quarter turn to the right, step onto the right foot.

26 Stomp the left foot.

▲ **27** Making a half turn to the left, step onto the left foot.

28 Stomp the right foot.

End standing on the left foot ready to start again. You are now facing the wall which was previously on you left.
The dance both starts and finishes with a Vine to the Right. Since there are two consecutive Vines to the Right, you could substitute a turn for one of them.
The Hip Swings can be modified to Hip Bumps. Hip Bumps can be used as an additional action to the Foot Taps Turning Left.

VINE TO THE RIGHT AND CLAP

29–31 Repeat Steps 1–3.

▶ **32** Close the left foot to the right foot and clap your hands.

I hope you have enjoyed learning the American Country Line Dances in this book and that you will enjoy them even more when you get onto the floor of your local Country & Western club for some foot stompin', boot scootin', toe tappin', knee hitchin', spur jinglin', honky tonkin', leather slappin', denim stretchin' fun. It's not what you do, it's the way that you do it, and if you're doing it with a sense of fun and are really enjoying yourself, then you're doing just great.

Style with Attitude

The tips below will help to further enhance your style with a little bit of "attitude." Attitude means exactly that – your frame of mind. If you feel inhibited, your dancing will reflect that, so let it go and put yourself in a positive frame of mind – it will show in your dance style.

During the dances, there is often room for improvisation, so that you can dance what you feel. This is perfectly acceptable, providing that the improvisation moves with the other dancers, it takes the same length of time as the original steps and leaves you on the correct foot and in an appropriate position to continue when you want to resume the routine.

I Feel Lucky includes a Turn to the Right and a Turn to the Left. You could replace a Vine to the Right or a Vine to the Left in other dances with these turns.

Turns can also be substituted for Backwards Walks. It is essential to be aware of the line of travel of the Backwards Walks, so that you can follow this line and avoid becoming disorientated and bumping into other dancers. In the Electric Slide, for example, the Backwards Walks start with the right foot. You can substitute turns which rotate clockwise, while moving back to end in the same position as if you had stuck to the original – you will be facing the front and standing on your right foot. Remember to keep your feet apart when you turn and to take small steps, as large ones will slow down the turn and unbalance you.

In the Electric Slide or any dance with Left Foot Forward Step Taps, why not lift your right foot a little higher and slap leather! Once you have got the idea of improvisation and feel comfortable, you could have some fun making up your own moves. Be careful not to put in so many substitutions that a dance becomes virtually a different dance, as this is off-putting to other dancers.

Generally, "attitude" is added to a move by allowing your own personality to express itself. Almost anything goes, and even simple enhancements such as slightly exaggerating the move can make your dancing look more dynamic. Try swapping a tap for a scuff or a stomp. Listen to the music and if it suggests something to you, try it. "You ain't gonna know till you give it a go!"

Further Information

Why not get in touch with your local dance school, or check your local clubs for organized Dance Ranches? Sharing and contributing to the pleasure of others as you learn American Country Line Dancing is not only much more rewarding, it's more fun for everyone, including you. The following organizations may be able to help with any additional enquiries about events:

The British Western Dance Association, 71 Sylvancroft, Ingol, Preston, Lancashire PR2 7BN, England

The Country Western Dance Council (UK), 8 Wick Lane, Flepham, Bognor Regis, West Sussex, PO22 8QG, England

Bootscooters International, P O Box 324, Leichardt, NSW, Australia

Acknowledgements

Many thanks to the following choreographers for their contribution to the enjoyment of Line Dancing: Gayle Brandon (Slappin' Leather), Linda DeFord (Ski Bumpus, Tennessee Twister), James Ferrazzano (Tush Push), Melanie Greenwood (The Achy Breaky) and Dennis Peterson (Boot Scootin' Boogie). The author would also like to acknowledge the many unknown choreographers who have contributed to the development of the dance.

The author and publishers would like to thank the following for their participation in the photography of this book. Their dance skills and enthusiasm were invaluable: Anny Ho, Katherine Porter, Ben Ryley, Shahriar Shariat amd Morwenna Wilson.

Jeans, shirts, props and accessories supplied by: American Classics Vintage Clothing, Bryan American World of Costumes and Props, Rancho Deluxe, Wrangler - The Authentic Western Jeans

Picture Credits

The Publishers would like to thank Super Stock for use of the image on page 6, and Sylvia Pitcher Photo Library for the image on page 7.